Hal•Leonard
INSTRUMENTAL
PLAY-ALONG

TENOR SAX

Boublil and Schönberg's

Les Misérables

Music by Claude-Michel Schönberg
Lyrics by Herbert Kretzmer
Original French Lyrics by Alain Boublil and J

T0081964

HOW TO USE THE CD ACCOMPANIMENT:
THE CD IS PLAYABLE ON ANY CD PLAYER. FOR PC AND MAC
USERS, THE CD IS ENHANCED SO YOU CAN ADJUST THE RECORD-
ING TO ANY TEMPO WITHOUT CHANGING PITCH.
A MELODY CUE APPEARS ON THE RIGHT CHANNEL ONLY. IF YOUR
CD PLAYER HAS A BALANCE ADJUSTMENT, YOU CAN ADJUST THE
VOLUME OF THE MELODY BY TURNING DOWN THE RIGHT CHANNEL.

ISBN 978-1-4234-3748-2

ALAIN BOUBLIL MUSIC LTD.
c/o Joel Faden and Company Inc.,
1775 Broadway, New York, NY 10019

HAL•LEONARD®
CORPORATION
7777 W. BLUEMOUND RD. P.O. BOX 13819 MILWAUKEE, WI 53213

Visit Hal Leonard Online at
www.halleonard.com

◆ AT THE END OF THE DAY

TENOR SAX

Music by CLAUDE-MICHEL SCHÖNBERG
Lyrics by ALAIN BOUBLIL, JEAN-MARC NATEL
and HERBERT KRETZMER

❖ BRING HIM HOME

TENOR SAX

Music by CLAUDE-MICHEL SCHÖNBERG
Lyrics by HERBERT KRETZMER and ALAIN BOUBLIL

❸ CASTLE ON A CLOUD

TENOR SAX

Music by CLAUDE-MICHEL SCHÖNBERG
Lyrics by ALAIN BOUBLIL, JEAN-MARC NATEL
and HERBERT KRETZMER

◆ DO YOU HEAR THE PEOPLE SING?

Music by CLAUDE-MICHEL SCHÖNBERG
Lyrics by ALAIN BOUBLIL, JEAN-MARC NATEL
and HERBERT KRETZMER

TENOR SAX

Music and Lyrics Copyright © 1980 by Editions Musicales Alain Boublil
English Lyrics Copyright © 1986 by Alain Boublil Music Ltd. (ASCAP)
Mechanical and Publication Rights for the U.S.A. Administered by Alain Boublil Music Ltd. (ASCAP)
c/o Stephen Tenenbaum & Co., Inc., 1775 Broadway, Suite 708, New York, NY 10019, Tel. (212) 246-7204, Fax (212) 246-7217

◆ DRINK WITH ME

(To Days Gone By)

TENOR SAX

Music by CLAUDE-MICHEL SCHÖNBERG
Lyrics by HERBERT KRETZMER and ALAIN BOUBLIL

❻ EMPTY CHAIRS AT EMPTY TABLES

TENOR SAX

Music by CLAUDE-MICHEL SCHÖNBERG
Lyrics by ALAIN BOUBLIL and HERBERT KRETZMER

❖7 A HEART FULL OF LOVE

TENOR SAX

Music by CLAUDE-MICHEL SCHÖNBERG
Lyrics by ALAIN BOUBLIL, JEAN-MARC NATEL
and HERBERT KRETZMER

❽ I DREAMED A DREAM

TENOR SAX

Music by CLAUDE-MICHEL SCHÖNBERG
Lyrics by ALAIN BOUBLIL, JEAN-MARC NATEL
and HERBERT KRETZMER

◆ 9 IN MY LIFE

TENOR SAX

Music by CLAUDE-MICHEL SCHÖNBERG
Lyrics by ALAIN BOUBLIL, JEAN-MARC NATEL
and HERBERT KRETZMER

rall.   a tempo

D.S. al Coda

CODA

rall.

🔟 A LITTLE FALL OF RAIN

TENOR SAX

Music by CLAUDE-MICHEL SCHÖNBERG
Lyrics by ALAIN BOUBLIL, JEAN-MARC NATEL
and HERBERT KRETZMER

◆ ON MY OWN

Music by CLAUDE-MICHEL SCHÖNBERG
Lyrics by ALAIN BOUBLIL, JEAN-MARC NATEL,
HERBERT KRETZMER, JOHN CAIRD
and TREVOR NUNN

TENOR SAX

⑫ STARS

TENOR SAX

Music by CLAUDE-MICHEL SCHÖNBERG
Lyrics by HERBERT KRETZMER and ALAIN BOUBLIL

⓭ WHO AM I?

TENOR SAX

Music by CLAUDE-MICHEL SCHÖNBERG
Lyrics by ALAIN BOUBLIL, JEAN-MARC NATEL
and HERBERT KRETZMER